FROM SEA to SHINING SEA

ALASKA

BARBARA A. SOMERVILL

Consultants

MELISSA N. MATUSEVICH, PH.D.
Curriculum and Instruction Specialist
Blacksburg, Virginia

KATY SPANGLER, PH.D.
Professor of Education
University of Alaska Southeast
Juneau, Alaska

CHILDREN'S PRESS ®
A DIVISION OF SCHOLASTIC INC.

New York • Toronto • London • Auckland • Sydney • Mexico City
New Delhi • Hong Kong • Danbury, Connecticut

Alaska is the northernmost state. It is surrounded by the Arctic Ocean, the Bering Sea, the Gulf of Alaska, and the Pacific Ocean. Alaska's land borders Canada to the east.

Project Editor: Meredith DeSousa
Art Director: Marie O'Neill
Photo Researcher: Marybeth Kavanagh
Design: Robin West, Ox and Company, Inc.
Page 6 map and recipe art: Susan Hunt Yule
All other maps: XNR Productions, Inc.

Library of Congress Cataloging-in-Publication Data

Somervill, Barbara A.
    Alaska / by Barbara Somervill.
      p.cm. – (From sea to shining sea)
    Includes bibliographical references (p.) and index.
    ISBN 0-516-22318-6
    1. Alaska – Juvenile literature. [1. Alaska.] I. Title. II.
From sea to shining sea (Series)

F904.3 .S66 2002
979.8—dc21   2001028877

TABLE of CONTENTS

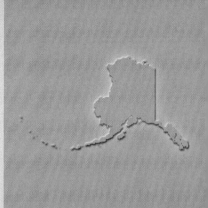

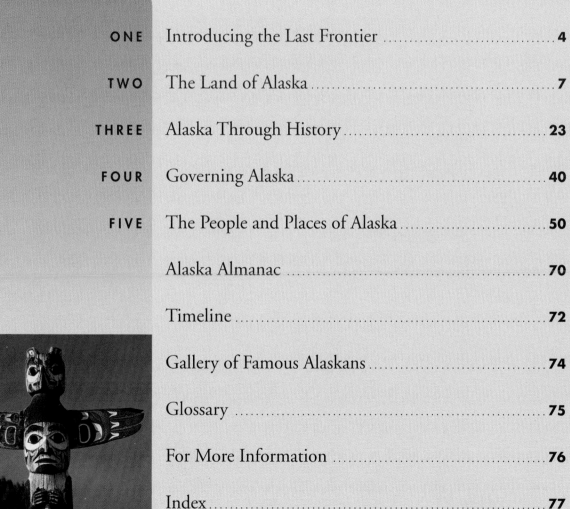

CHAPTER

CHAPTER ONE

INTRODUCING THE LAST FRONTIER

Breathtaking scenery and peaceful moments are part of everyday life in many parts of Alaska.

You **might think that the "last frontier"** is the deepest part of the ocean or the farthest star in outer space. For the United States, the "last frontier" is Alaska. This rugged, sparsely populated, and beautiful state is known as the Last Frontier because it contains some of the last areas of unsettled wilderness in the world.

If you were to place a map of Alaska on a map of the lower forty-eight states, Alaska would reach across from San Francisco to Cleveland. Alaska measures 2,700 miles (4,345 kilometers) east to west—from its eastern Canadian border to the farthest Aleutian Islands in the Pacific Ocean. From north to south, Alaska measures 1,400 miles (2,253 km)—from Point Barrow far above the Arctic Circle to Unimak Island in the Pacific Ocean.

Alaska is not only the largest state, it is also one of the most unusual. The land is full of extremes, from cold desert tundra to volcanoes to rainforests. In the northern part of the state, the tilt of the earth results in summer months of continuous daylight and winter months of total darkness. Alaska has the third smallest population of all the states-only Vermont and Wyoming have fewer people. In contrast, Alaska is home to millions of wild animals, including bears, caribou, moose, whales, salmon—and mosquitoes!

The story of Alaska's flag is fascinating. In 1926, the Alaskan territory held a flag-designing contest among junior high school and high school students. The winner was thirteen-year-old Benny Benson, whose simple design featured eight gold stars—representing the North Star and the Big Dipper—against a dark blue background. The North Star represented the northernmost part of the United States, and the Big Dipper stood for strength. People liked the flag so much that when Alaska became a state in 1959, they voted to keep it as the official state flag.

What comes to mind when you think of Alaska?

❖ The Iditarod dogsled races from Anchorage to Nome
❖ Caribou grazing on the tundra
❖ Alaska Natives hunting and fishing
❖ Sourdoughs panning for gold
❖ Humpback whales off the coast of Alaska
❖ Ships and buses full of tourists visiting Juneau or Denali National Park
❖ The colored lights of the aurora borealis flowing across the night sky
❖ Thousands of beautiful glaciers, rivers, and lakes

Alaska is a place of many contrasts. Alaska is a mix of modern cities and wilderness; a land of long winters with dark days, and short summers when the sun hardly sets. In this book, you'll read about the people, places, and events of the Last Frontier.

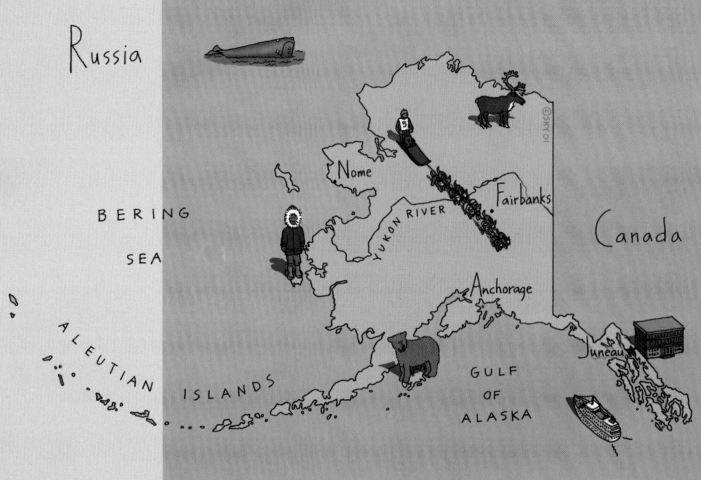

ARCTIC OCEAN

Russia

BERING

SEA

ALEUTIAN ISLANDS

Nome

Fairbanks

YUKON RIVER

Anchorage

Canada

Juneau

GULF
OF
ALASKA

PACIFIC OCEAN

CHAPTER TWO

THE LAND OF ALASKA

Alaska is the largest state by far. It is more than twice the size of Texas and almost 500 times the size of Rhode Island. In fact, Alaska covers 615,230 square miles (1,593,438 square kilometers). Of that area, 570,374 square miles (1,477,269 sq km) is land. That means that Alaska contains 44,856 square miles (116,177 sq km) of lakes and rivers!

To the east, Alaska shares a 1,150-mile (1,850-km) boundary with British Columbia and the Yukon Territory of Canada. To the west lies the Pacific Ocean, and further west, Russia. The Arctic Ocean is to the north of Alaska, and the Gulf of Alaska is to the south.

The state's northern extreme, Point Barrow, lies about 350 miles (563 km) above the Arctic Circle. The Aleutian Islands, which are also part of Alaska, cut an arc far south and west into the Pacific. One of Alaska's islands in the Bering Sea is Little Diomede, which is only about 2.5 miles (4 km) from Russia's Big Diomede Island.

Portions of the Chugach Mountains in southcentral Alaska are covered with glaciers.

7

THE REGIONS OF ALASKA

Alaskans divide their state into six regions. They are the North Slope, Western Alaska, the Aleutian region, the Interior, Southcentral Alaska, and Southeast Alaska. These regions are determined by unique geographic characteristics and by the original Alaska Native cultures that are found in each region.

The North Slope

The tundra is familiar scenery on the North Slope.

The North Slope, or Arctic Coastal Plain, gently slopes to the Arctic Ocean and the Beaufort Sea in the north from the foothills of the Brooks Range. The entire North Slope is located within the Arctic Circle,

the region around the North Pole. The Arctic Circle is an imaginary line drawn around the earth's surface at approximately 66° 30'N. This is truly the "land of the midnight sun." Barrow is the largest town in this region.

Treeless tundra covers most of the North Slope. In the tundra, a layer of permanently frozen soil called permafrost lies just below a thin top layer of soil. Even in the summer, the tundra never gets very warm, so the permafrost doesn't melt. Water cannot drain deep into the soil, making the tundra's surface very spongy and delicate. In some places the land is frozen to a depth of more than 2,000 feet (610 meters). There is very little precipitation in the tundra. Along the northern coast, the sea freezes hard. People and polar bears take advantage of hard ice to fish or hunt.

Mosses and lichens cover the spongy tundra soil. Berry bushes, willows, and grasses bloom during summer. Millions of migrating birds nest in the North Slope. The tundra is the perfect home for caribou, polar bears, and smaller mammals, while the ocean supports whales, seals, and walruses. Oil, found just offshore of the North Slope, is a valuable natural resource.

Western Alaska

Western Alaska juts out into the Bering Sea. It includes the Seward Peninsula in the north and the vast Yukon and Kuskokwim River deltas. Western Alaska contains some mountain ranges, however, much of the land is wet, flat lowland. Since Western Alaska borders the Pacific

Ocean, the weather is wet and often very windy. Nome, Bethel, and Dillingham are the largest towns in this region.

Thousands of lakes cover Western Alaska. Many are so small that they do not have names. The Yukon River drains into Norton Sound, and the Kuskokwim River meets the ocean at Kuskokwim Bay. Both of these great rivers meander, meaning that they are slow moving, with many twists and branches, through the lowlands. These wetlands form part of one of the largest wildlife refuges in the United States, the Yukon Delta National Wildlife Refuge.

Located on the Seward Peninsula, the Bering Land Bridge National Preserve is what remains of the original land bridge that connected Asia with North America thousands of years ago. The Yukon-Charley Rivers National Preserve protects more than 100 miles (160 km) of the Yukon River and the entire Charley River basin.

This river is thick with salmon.

Western Alaska also includes several islands. Little Diomede Island, west of the Seward Peninsula, is just a few miles from the border of Russia. Nunivak Island in the Bering Sea shelters a large herd of musk ox.

Millions of birds nest and breed in Western Alaska's wetlands. Caribou and moose make their homes here. In addition, five species of Pacific salmon swim into the rivers of western Alaska to spawn, or reproduce. These are the largest schools of wild salmon in the world.

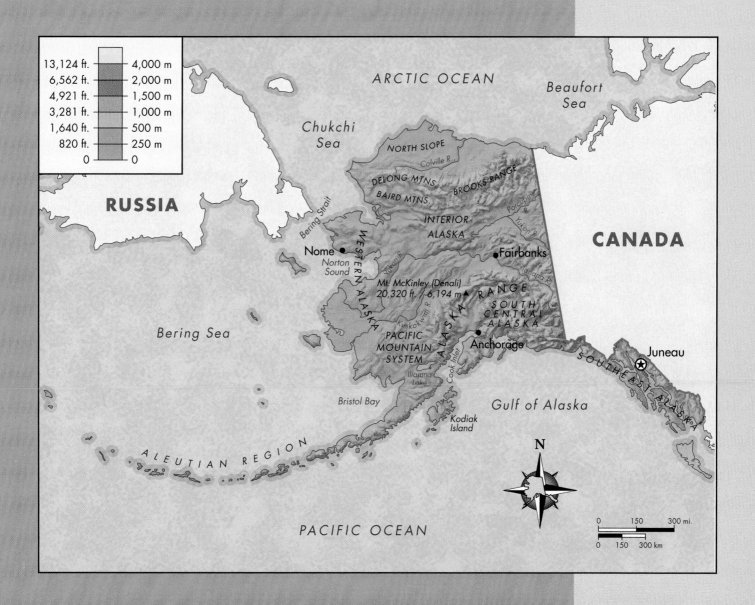

ARCTIC OCEAN

Beaufort
Sea

Chukchi
Sea

NORTH SLOPE

Colville R.

DELONG MTNS.

BROOKS RANGE

BAIRD MTNS.

INTERIOR
ALASKA

Porcupine R.

Yukon R.

CANADA

Bering Strait

Nome

Norton
Sound

WESTERN ALASKA

Fairbanks

Mt. McKinley (Denali)
20,320 ft. / 6,194 m

ALASKA RANGE

SOUTH
CENTRAL
ALASKA

Tanana R.

RUSSIA

Bering Sea

Kuskokwim R.

PACIFIC
MOUNTAIN
SYSTEM

Anchorage

Cook Inlet

Juneau

SOUTHEAST ALASKA

Iliamna
Lake

Bristol Bay

Gulf of Alaska

Kodiak
Island

ALEUTIAN REGION

PACIFIC OCEAN

13,124 ft. — 4,000 m
6,562 ft. — 2,000 m
4,921 ft. — 1,500 m
3,281 ft. — 1,000 m
1,640 ft. — 500 m
820 ft. — 250 m
0 — 0

N

0   150   300 mi.
0   150   300 km

The Aleutian Region

The Aleutian region includes the Aleutian Chain and the Alaska Peninsula, which stretch in a long, curving line about 1,400 miles (2,240 km) into the Pacific Ocean. The Aleutian Islands are a row of more than 150 small islands and mark the southern boundary of the Bering Sea. Unalaska, just off the Alaska Peninsula, is the eastern border of the Aleutian Chain. The farthest island to the west, Attu Island, is actually in the Eastern Hemisphere. The Pribilof Islands to the north of the Aleutians are also considered part of the Aleutian Chain.

The Aleutians make up part of the ring of volcanoes and unstable land that forms the Pacific Ring of Fire around the Pacific Ocean. Although it was formed by volcanic eruptions long ago, most of the Aleutians today are small, rounded, treeless islands with rocky shores. Constant winds bend the grasses and low lying plants.

The Aleutians make perfect nesting grounds for puffins and other sea birds. The rocky shorelines of the Aleutians once swarmed with sea otters and seals. Three of every four northern fur seals live on the Pribilof Islands. Today, these animals are protected from commercial harvest.

Interior Alaska

The central region of Alaska is called the Interior. Mountain ranges form two of this region's borders: to the south, the Alaska Range; and to the north, the Brooks Range,

FIND OUT MORE

The earth is divided into halves, called hemispheres, going east/west, and north/south. The Northern Hemisphere is the half between the North Pole and the equator, and the Southern Hemisphere is between the South Pole and the equator. Find out how the Earth is divided east and west. In which hemisphere is most of the United States located?

the northernmost tip of the Rocky Mountains. To the west is Western Alaska, and the east forms a border with Canada. The climate is dry and extreme. The hottest and coldest temperatures in Alaska have been recorded in the Interior.

This area of low, rolling hills is the largest region of Alaska and contains one of the state's largest cities, Fairbanks. Several of the state's major rivers flow through the Interior, including the Yukon, Kuskokwim, and Tanana Rivers.

North America's highest mountain, Denali (meaning "the great one"), lies within the Alaska Mountain Range. Denali is 20,320 feet (6,194 m) high. After President McKinley died, the mountain was renamed Mount McKinley. In 1975, Alaskans returned to using the name Denali for the mountain and its surrounding national park.

Within the the Brooks Range is the Arctic National Wildlife Refuge (ANWR), home to a herd

Denali is the highest point in North America.

WHO'S WHO IN ALASKA?

Hudson Stuck (1865–1920) and his three companions climbed Denali in 1913, becoming the first people of European descent to reach its tallest peak. Stuck was an Episcopalian priest and writer who worked to preserve Alaska's native traditions. He was born in London, England, and later lived in Alaska.

of about 110,000 caribou. This herd migrates throughout the refuge. Other animals living within the Brooks Range include grizzly bears and gray wolves. More than 175 varieties of birds build summer nests in the refuge.

Taiga forests, thin forests of birch and spruce trees, cover much of the Interior. The trees are short and widely spaced because the topsoil above the permafrost is so thin. Blueberries cover many mountain slopes in the Interior. Gold, silver, and platinum are important minerals found in this area.

Caribou graze on the Alaskan tundra.

Southcentral Alaska

Just above the Gulf of Alaska lies Southcentral Alaska. Simply called "Southcentral" by Alaskans, this region is the most densely populated part of Alaska. It includes the Anchorage area, the Matanuska-Susitna Valleys, the Kenai Peninsula, Kodiak Island, and the Prince William Sound shoreline. Anchorage, the largest city in Alaska, is more than eight times the size of the next largest cities, Juneau and Fairbanks, and has almost a third of the state's entire population.

Southcentral Alaska has a milder climate than the Interior because it is further south and borders the ocean. However, the further a person travels from the coast, the more extreme the climate becomes. Much of Southcentral is mountainous, providing habitats for mountain goats and Dall sheep. Area rivers often look gray because they contain the silt of Southcentral's many glaciers. The rugged coastline includes many islands. Bears and moose are common in Southcentral, and often appear in neighborhood backyards. The Kenai River is famous for its run of Chinook, or king, salmon, the world's largest salmon.

Much of Southcentral is covered with boreal, thick forests of spruce, birch, and willow. At higher elevations, the forest becomes alpine tundra. The largest state park in the United States, Chugach Park, is a playground for Southcentral residents. The Matanuska-Susitna Valley has excellent farmland and produces giant vegetables grown during the long summer days. Far to the east lies the Wrangell-St. Elias National Park, the largest national park in the country. The region is also home to ten active volcanoes. The most recent eruption was in 1992 at Mount Spurr. Volcano damage was not severe because the volcano lies in a remote area.

The cool, rainy climate of Tongass National Forest makes it the perfect home for a variety of plants, animals, and birds.

Southeast Alaska

Southeast Alaska, or "the Panhandle," is the narrow strip of mountains and islands that stretches down to the southeast. British Columbia, Canada, forms the eastern border of this region. The Pacific Ocean lies to the west. Many towns in Southeast cannot be reached by road or train—the Alaska Marine Highway system of ferries serves towns such as the

state capital, Juneau, as well as Sitka and Ketchikan. Southeast Alaska, which includes about one thousand islands, is the most visited part of Alaska.

Southeast Alaska has a wet marine climate. Because of the warmer temperatures and frequent rainfall, the forests of Southeast Alaska differ from the rest of the state. Sitka spruce, western hemlock, and cedar trees tower over the mosses and ferns of the dense forest floor. Logging is a major local industry. Rugged shorelines meet mountains that seem to rise directly from the sea. Animals thrive, including black bear, deer, and birds. Seals, whales, and countless fish swim just offshore. Gold and copper are commonly found in Southeast Alaska.

WATER AND ICE

Alaska has more inland water than any other state. It has more than three million lakes, three thousand rivers, and a shoreline that includes the Gulf of Alaska, as well as many straits, bays, and sounds. Some of Alaska's water, however, is locked in ice at least part of the year.

The Yukon River is the longest river in Alaska. It flows from the Yukon Territory in Canada to the east and empties into the Norton Sound in the west. The Yukon River is 1,979 miles (3,184 km) long, but only 1,265 miles (2,036 km) are in Alaska. Several major Alaskan rivers feed into the Yukon, including the Porcupine, the Koyukuk, and the Tanana Rivers. Other big rivers in the state include the Kuskokwim,

Skilak Lake, shown here, is just one of Alaska's millions of lakes.

the Kobuk, and the Noatak. The Colville River flows into the Arctic Ocean. The Susitna, Copper, and Kenai river systems in Southcentral Alaska are famous for their salmon runs.

Alaska has more than three million lakes, many of which are always frozen. Iliamna Lake, in the southwestern part of the state, is Alaska's largest lake. It covers 1,150 square miles (2,978 sq km).

The state also has more than five thousand glaciers—large bodies of ice formed from closely packed snow. Malaspina and Bering Glaciers are the two largest, each covering about 2,300 square miles (5,957 sq km) of land. You could put the state of Rhode Island inside one of these

These campers are admiring the spectacular Mendenhall Glacier.

glaciers and still have room left over. Many glaciers are near roads and are easy to visit. These include the Worthington, Matanuska, Portage, and Mendenhall Glaciers.

CLIMATE

Alaska has varied weather conditions around the state. Thanks to lower latitude and the warm winds blowing from the Pacific Ocean, the

Alaska Panhandle has a milder climate then the northern part of the state. The Interior of Alaska gets the coldest temperatures in winter and the warmest in the summer. Northern Alaska has bitterly cold winters and cool summers.

Alaskan winters are long and dark. Snow falls as early as September and may still be on the ground in April or May. Temperatures on winter days are usually below freezing. The average January temperature across the state is 5° Fahrenheit (–15° Celsius). The record low temperature is –80°F (–62°C), which occurred at Prospect Creek on January 23, 1971. Frostbite (skin or muscle damage from intense cold) and hypothermia (loss of body heat) are serious problems for people who spend a lot of time outdoors in Alaska's winter weather. Alaskans must also be aware of the winds, or wind chill factor, which make the low temperatures seem even colder.

Alaskans love summer because the days are long and often sunny. The average July temperature is 54°F (12°C), although it can reach anywhere from 60°F (16°C) to 90°F (32°C) in the summer in some parts of the state. The highest recorded temperature in Alaska is 100°F (38°C) at Fort Yukon on June 27, 1915.

On average, Alaska receives 56 inches (142 centimeters) of precipitation—rain, snow, or sleet—each year, although some parts of the state get more precipitation than

EXTRA! EXTRA!

For Alaska Natives, nature has been both a close friend and a respected enemy. As a result, native people have dozens of names for different kinds of snow, such as old snow, fresh snow, snowflake, fluffy snow, and packed snow. There are also several names for the Alaskan winds. The Chinook is a warm wind that brings an early winter thaw. The Taku is a cold, Arctic wind that can reach up to 100 miles an hour (161 km per hour). Williwaws are sudden, strong gusts of wind.

Even longtime Alaskans are fascinated by the northern lights dancing in the night sky.

others. Specifically, the northern part of the panhandle averages about 220 inches (559 cm) of precipitation, while the North Slope receives as little as 10 inches (25.4 cm) per year.

An exciting event in the Alaskan skies is the aurora borealis, or northern lights. Electrical discharges in the earth's atmosphere, called solar winds, create red, green, and purple lights that burst through the night skies near the Arctic Circle. The lights dance and sway, fold and unfold, and ripple like a curtain in the sky. Fairbanks is a great place to see the northern lights, especially in the spring and fall.

PLANTS AND ANIMALS

Roughly one-fourth of Alaska is forested. In the Interior, the forest is called taiga—a thin forest of birch and spruce. Further south, boreal is a thicker forest with larger spruce trees, tall birches, and cottonwoods. Alder, spruce, cedar, and hemlock trees grow in the Southeast Alaska rain forest. Alaska has many types of willow, from low bushes to small leafy trees. Some woodlands are filled with wild asters, violets, cowslips, lupines, and larkspur, and the highways often are lined with fireweed during the summer months. The state also has more than five hundred types of wild mushrooms. Alaska's wild berries include lingonberries, blueberries, cranberries, and strawberries, as well as more unusual types such as nagoonberries, crowberries, and soapberries.

Although hundreds of animal species are found in Alaska, the state is best known for its bears. The gigantic Kodiak bear, found on Kodiak Island, grows to 1,500 pounds (682 kilograms). When

A Kodiak bear tries to catch fish for dinner.

standing on their hind legs, Kodiak bears loom more than 10 feet (3 m) tall. The Kodiak bear is a variety of brown or grizzly bear. Bears gain needed weight to endure winter hibernation by eating large amounts of salmon. The Alaskan brown bear and the black bear are superb salmon fishers. The massive polar bear travels the tundra and solid ice along the northern and western coast, looking for ringed seals to eat. Polar bears are strong swimmers and can tow their cubs behind them through 50 miles (80 km) of icy Arctic waters.

Fifteen species of whales live in Alaskan waters. Humpback, blue, bowhead, northern right, finback, sei, minke, and gray whales are common, as are orcas. California gray whales migrate 10,000 miles (16,093 km) round trip each year, from the Bering Sea to Baja California.

Warm summer weather finds Alaska alive with birds. Golden plovers travel from their winter nests in Hawaii to Alaska each spring. Arctic terns that nest in the area during the summer migrate 10,000 miles (16,090 km) to Antarctica, where they live from October through April. Millions of ducks, Canada geese, snow geese, and trumpeter swans summer in the Copper River Delta, near Cordova. More bald eagles nest along the Chilkat River in Southeast Alaska than any other place in the world.

Humpback whales can often be seen swimming off the southern Alaska coast. Their extremely long fins set them apart from other whales.

CHAPTER THREE

ALASKA THROUGH HISTORY

About forty thousand years ago, glaciers, or large masses of ice, spread across North America. As the glaciers grew, they took water from the oceans and seas, leaving dry land. The lower water level exposed land connecting Asia and North America. This created a bridge between the two continents, called the Bering Land Bridge. This dry land included the seafloor of the Bering Strait and most of the Chukchi Sea.

People called Paleo-Indians, who lived between thirty thousand and ten thousand years ago, probably walked across the land bridge into what is now Alaska. These first Alaskans were the ancestors of three main Native American groups: the Aleut, the Inuit, and the Alaskan Indians. All three groups were hunter-gatherers. They hunted seals, whales, fish, and caribou; and gathered roots, berries, and nuts.

In the late 1800s and early 1900s, Alaska was a hot spot for gold miners.

23

The Inuit people spread out across the northern and western regions of Alaska. The Aleut settled mainly on a string of islands called the Aleutians. The Aleut lived close to the sea, surviving by hunting and fishing.

Many native people hunted and traveled on the icy seas of Alaska. The Aleut made a kayak called a *baidarka*, using seal skins to keep the boat waterproof. The Inuit made canoe-like boats called *umiaks* by stretching walrus skins over a driftwood frame. With these boats, hunters traveled far out to sea to catch whales, seals, and walruses.

On land, Alaska Natives traveled long distances by using dogsleds. The sleds were made of driftwood and animal bones that were lashed together with animal skins. Harnesses for the dogs were made using caribou or reindeer hides.

Alaskan Indians were not related to the Inuit or the Aleut. They belonged to several different tribes. They are the Athabascan, the Tlingit, the Haida, and the Tsimshian. The Athabascan lived in the interior of Alaska. They gathered nuts and berries, hunted for game, and fished in Alaska's many rivers. The Haida, Tsimshian, and Tlingit settled along Alaska's Panhandle. These three tribes depended on fishing for their main food supply.

Alaska Natives used dog-sleds as a means of travel.

Alaska Natives lived off the land. To show their respect for animals, they used every part of each animal they killed. Meat was eaten immediately, or dried or smoked for later meals. Fat was used for cooking, oil lamps, and waterproofing. Bones were used to make eating utensils, buttons, fishhooks, sewing needles, and tools. Skins were used for clothing, making boats, lining floors and walls of homes, shoes, and so on. Nothing was ever wasted.

THE RUSSIANS ARRIVE IN ALASKA

In 1741, explorer Vitus Bering sailed under orders from Peter the Great, czar of Russia. Bering's mission was to map the eastern coast of Russia and the north Pacific Ocean. Bering and his men came close enough to see Mount St. Elias and land on Kayak Island in the Gulf of Alaska. The explorers were shipwrecked on their way home and were left stranded on an island, now named Bering Island. Bering and many of his men died of cold and disease.

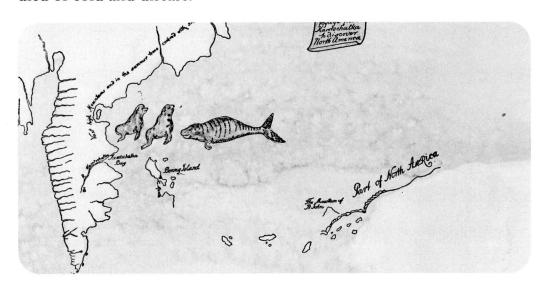

A member of Vitus Bering's crew drew this map of the area. The symbols indicated a wealth of sea otters.

The few survivors eventually took their cargo of sea otter furs back to Russia. Furs were considered a valuable resource at the time and were worth a lot of money. After news of the rich fur supply spread, Europeans, Asians, and North Americans came to Alaska looking for quick wealth. The first to arrive were the Russians. In 1784, Russian fur trader Grigori Shelekhov established the first European settlement on Kodiak Island. The settlement was moved to Kodiak village in 1792 and grew to become a center of Russian fur trading.

As more money was made, the Russians needed more and more furs to keep the business going. Often they kidnapped Alaska Natives who were skilled hunters. The natives became slaves—they were controlled and owned by the Russians, who forced them to work without pay. They were treated poorly, and many of them eventually died from cruel treatment and disease.

Sitka, originally called New Archangel, served as the first capital of Russian America.

In 1799, Russian Alexandr Baranov founded a fur trading post at New Archangel (later renamed Sitka) for the Russian-American Company. The Tlingits already occupied the land around New Archangel, and they did not welcome the arrival of the Russians. In 1802, the Tlingit attacked the trading post and killed most of the 450 Russians living there.

Baranov was away from the settlement at the time. Two years later, Baranov returned and reclaimed the area for Russia. Sitka was rebuilt and named the capital of Russian America. For the next sixty-five years, the Russians controlled much of Alaska.

ENGLISH AND SPANISH EXPLORATION

As the Russians developed their trading posts, England and Spain also wanted a piece of Alaska. In 1778, Captain James Cook became the first English explorer to sail the North Pacific and the Chukchi Sea. Fourteen years later, George Vancouver explored and mapped Alaska's southeast region as far as Cook Inlet, near present-day Anchorage. Vancouver had served under Captain Cook and knew the area from earlier travels. Vancouver named several Alaskan sites with British names: Cook Inlet, Prince William Sound, and Prince of Wales Island.

The Spanish were also interested in Alaska. In 1773, explorer Juan Perez sailed in the area. However, Perez did not set up a land base. The Spanish regarded their claims to Mexico and California as going all the way to Alaska.

More Spanish ships arrived in Alaska in 1787. Spain and Great Britain almost went to war over Alaskan land. Spain finally gave up its dealings in Alaskan territory in 1792. However, Spanish names for Alaskan sites remained, such as Malaspina Glacier, Valdez, Cordova, and Pedro Bay.

English explorer Captain James Cook made maps of the American northwest coast.

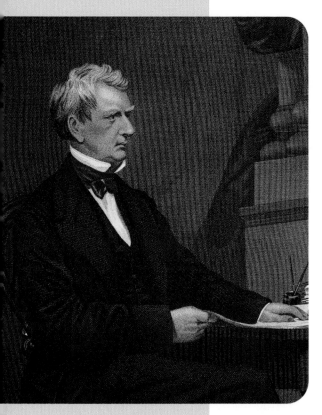

Secretary of State William Seward negotiated the purchase of Alaska from Russia.

By the mid-1850s, the Alaskan fur trade had slowed down because fur was no longer in great demand. In 1867, the Russians agreed to sell Alaska to the United States. United States Secretary of State William Seward made a deal to buy Alaska for $7.2 million, about two cents an acre. The American flag flew over Alaska for the first time on October 18, 1867. Although many Americans thought Seward's purchase was a foolish one, history would soon show that it turned out to be a bargain for the United States.

In the beginning, the United States government paid little attention to Alaska. The Civil War had recently ended, and the government's first concern was rebuilding the South. Between war debts and Reconstruction, there was little money left over for Alaska. However, the citizens of Alaska knew that they needed a form of government and continued to ask Congress for help.

In 1884, the United States Congress passed the First Organic Act, which created the District of Alaska. This act set up a government in Alaska and established a school system for Alaska's children. A handful of government officials were appointed by the president, but they had little success governing a territory the size of Alaska. The act did not provide for the collection of taxes or set up land laws. Although the Organic Act was a step in the right direction, it was simply not enough.

GOLD RUSH

In 1880, Joseph Juneau, Richard Harris, and three Tlingit guides discovered gold in southeastern Alaska. Their discovery led to the founding of Juneau. The big gold rush, however, came in 1896, when gold was found in the Yukon region of Canada, just across the border from Alaska.

News of the gold strikes spread around the world, and, in the years that followed, many people rushed to Alaska and the Yukon to mine for gold. Towns were hastily constructed around the meeting point of the Yukon and Klondike Rivers in Canada. Soon, more gold was found along the Tanana River, in Nome, and in Fairbanks. Cities that were only collections of tents sprang up almost overnight all around Alaska. These miners hoped to get rich quick by staking claims and panning for gold.

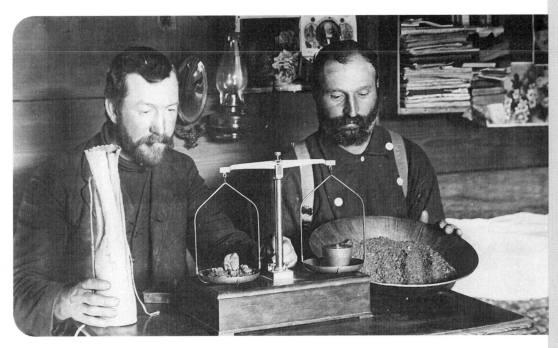

These men are using a scale to weigh gold nuggets.

However, real life was very different. Few miners realized how difficult it would be to live in Alaska. Frostbitten fingers and toes created problems during icy winter months. Flies and mosquitoes swarmed the mining camps during the summer. Miners worried about dangerous animals, such as bears or wolves, that might attack their camps. They also feared having their mining land stolen by other men. Someone might file a claim on land that another person had already claimed. This type of theft was called claim-jumping.

The arrival of miners and prospectors also brought businesspeople who made fortunes selling clothes, tents, food, and tools to those miners. The cities of Nome, Juneau, and Fairbanks were founded as supply posts for miners on their way to the gold fields. In 1900, Juneau became the new capital.

In the gold rush days, some tent cities, like this one in Nome, eventually developed into cities and towns.

An explosion in Alaska's population followed the discovery of gold. Before the gold rush, about 32,000 people lived there. By 1900, the population climbed to more than 63,000—almost double. The population explosion created some serious problems in Alaska. Claim-jumping, theft, murder (usually over gold mining claims), and many other crimes were common. Alaska needed both laws and people to enforce those laws.

As the gold mines developed, it was necessary to find ways to reach mining towns and deliver mail and supplies. Many towns could be served by steamboats, but rivers froze in winter, making water travel impossible. A dogsled trail, open through the winter, provided a solution. The original trail went from Seward on the Kenai Peninsula to Nome in the west. Drivers, called mushers, drove teams of twenty or more dogs pulling sleds full of freight. Dogsleds carried up to a half-ton of weight.

ALASKA, THE TERRITORY

In 1912, Congress officially made Alaska a United States territory. The territory needed new roads, new schools, and public buildings. A railroad line was a necessity. Construction of the Alaska Railroad began in 1914 and eventually linked Seward and Anchorage to Fairbanks in the interior.

As the Alaska Railroad was being built, a tent city of two thousand people grew along the coast of Cook Inlet. What began as a railroad construction town blossomed into Alaska's largest city, Anchorage. Stores opened, businesses were started, and more people arrived. By the time the railroad was completed in 1923, Anchorage was on its way to becoming the business center of Alaska. Slow growth would continue for the next twenty years.

WORLD WAR II AND STATEHOOD

In 1941, the United States entered World War II (1939–1945) and fought against Japan, Germany, Italy, and other countries. On June 3, 1942, the Japanese dropped bombs on Dutch Harbor in the Aleutians. Then, the Japanese took over two islands, Attu and Kiska—the only North American soil that was occupied by an enemy force during World War II.

The United States quickly realized that a road was needed to bring troops and supplies to Alaska. Army engineers attacked the problem of building a road from Washington state through Canada to Alaska. This road was first called the Alaska-Canada Highway, but was later shortened to the Alcan Highway. The highway was needed so urgently that it was built in only eight months at a rate of almost two hundred miles (322 km) a month!

To protect the Aleuts from further Japanese attacks, the United States Army removed the Aleuts from their homes in the Aleutian Islands. The Aleuts were forced to leave their homes at a minute's notice, with hardly any belongings. The military crammed them onto ships and transported them to Southeast Alaska. There, they lived in run-down camps with little food, no electricity, and no medical care. Many Aleuts

This World War II Japanese freighter still lies in the waters off Kiska.

died as a result of the poor living conditions. In May 1943, United States forces landed on Attu and reclaimed American land from the Japanese. At the end of the war, the United States government finally allowed the Aleuts to return home.

By the time World War II ended, Alaska's population had reached 112,000. The territory applied for statehood. In 1955, fifty-five Alaskans met to write a state constitution, a document that outlines the basic rules and

WHO'S WHO IN ALASKA?

Elizabeth Peratrovich (1911–1958) was a Tlingit who fought to end discrimination, or unfair treatment, against Alaska Natives. In the early 1900s, many whites tried to separate Alaska Natives from the rest of society by not allowing them to enter stores and seating them in separate sections of movie theaters and restaurants. Elizabeth's efforts ultimately led to the passing of the Anti-Discrimination Act in 1945, a law that made discrimination illegal. Today, Alaskans celebrate Elizabeth Peratrovich Day every February 16th. She was born in Petersburg.

On June 30, 1958, the Anchorage newspaper triumphantly announced that the United States Senate had voted in favor of statehood.

laws by which a government is run. They were planning ahead for statehood.

Once the constitution was approved, the United States House of Representatives and the Senate passed an act that allowed Alaska to become a state. On August 26, 1958, Alaskans voted five to one in favor of statehood. On January 3, 1959, President Dwight Eisenhower signed a law and Alaska officially became the forty-ninth state. Another star was added to the United States flag. William Egan served as the first governor of the state of Alaska.

THE MIGHTY LAND OF ALASKA

On March 27, 1964, a massive earthquake (one of the strongest ever recorded) rocked Anchorage. Although it only lasted between three and five minutes, property damage to the state was in the millions. People lost homes, businesses, and personal items. The sudden uplift of the ocean floor also caused a giant tidal wave, called a tsunami, that destroyed neighboring towns such as Valdez. The earthquake was felt over a large area of southcentral Alaska and in the Canadian Yukon. More than one hundred people died as a result of the earthquake and tsunami.

In 1968, the big news in Alaska was the discovery of oil at Prudhoe Bay on the North Slope. The Prudhoe Bay oil and natural gas deposit was considered a major find. The only problem was transporting the oil from Prudhoe Bay, which is about three hundred miles (480 km) north of the Arctic Circle, to a port on the Gulf of Alaska that was open all year. The answer to this problem was the Trans-Alaska Pipeline, completed in 1977. The pipeline runs eight hundred miles (1,287 km) through Alaska, crossing three mountain ranges and hundreds of rivers and streams. Hot oil runs through the pipeline all the way from northern Alaska to Valdez in the south, where it can then be shipped to the lower 48 states.

The pipeline cost $8 billion to build. However, the oil deposit was rich, and the state sold drilling rights to oil companies. Payment for the oil and transportation provided the state with a great deal of money. It was so successful that Alaskans stopped paying state

During the 1964 earthquake in Anchorage, people saw houses sink into the ground, cracks open up beneath their feet, and trees collapse. The city was rebuilt after the earthquake.

WHAT'S IN A NAME?

Many names of places in Alaska have interesting origins.

Name	Comes From or Means
Alaska	From the Aleut *al-ay-es-ka*, meaning "great land"
Juneau	After Joe Juneau, gold miner
Seward	After William Seward, who arranged for the United States to buy Alaska from Russia
Denali	Athabascan word for "the great one"
Prince of Wales Island	Named by Vancouver for British Royalty
Valdez	Named by the Spanish, a last name
Bering	After the Danish explorer, Vitus Bering
Baranof Island	After Alexandr Baranov, governor of Russian Alaska

The Trans-Alaska pipeline traverses some of Alaska's most beautiful scenery.

income tax and collected an oil "bonus" payment instead.

Despite its success, the business of producing oil sometimes causes problems. In 1989, the oil tanker *Exxon Valdez* ran aground and spilled eleven million gallons of oil into Prince William Sound. The spill destroyed birds, mammals, and fish in the sound. In 1991, Exxon was fined $900 million to pay for the problems caused by the oil spill and the cleanup.

36

Although the discovery of oil on the North Slope helped many people, it was also considered a threat to the preservation of Alaska Native land. For many years, Alaska's native people fought to keep their land and preserve Alaska's natural resources. The discovery of oil and the large number of national parks and preserves cut into native lands. The native people protested, asking to be paid for the use of resources taken over by business and government.

The *Exxon Valdez* disaster was the largest oil spill in United States history. The remote location of the spill made cleanup efforts extremely difficult.

In 1971, the U.S. Congress passed the Alaska Native Claims Settlement Act (ANCSA). This law gave 44 million acres (18 million hectares) of Alaskan land and $962.5 million to Alaska's native people. The law stated that groups of natives must form companies or corporations to control the land and money. Today, these corporations own and operate fisheries, canneries, lumber mills, and mines (coal, tin, gold, platinum, iron ore, jade, and silver).

A long-standing problem for Alaskans—both native and non-native—is subsistence. This refers to hunting and fishing for food, clothing (made from skins or furs), and home goods (animal hides used for sleeping mats or bones used for making tools). Alaska natives, in particular, view subsistence living as a way of life. Store-bought food is very expensive in small native villages, and money is short. Many families would starve without subsistence living.

Subsistence for most native families means hunting walrus, whales, seals, and caribou. One walrus, for example, provides three meals a day for more than a month, as well as hide for making boats, blubber for fuel oil, and ivory for crafts. Natives use the bones for making tools. Ideally, no part of the animal goes to waste. Hunting walrus, whales, and seals falls under the Marine Mammals Protection Act, which allows only native people to hunt these creatures. Natives also hunt caribou and use the meat, hide, bones, and hooves much as they have done for centuries.

Fishing supports the subsistence lifestyle. Recently, building roads into rural areas and commercial fishing have threatened native fishing rights. State officials also tried to close down some subsistence fishing sites. This encouraged Alaska Native Katie John to file a lawsuit against the state government in 1991. The court battle continues today as to how subsistence should best be protected for the good of all Alaskans.

Throughout the 1990s, Alaska's natural environment presented problems. In 1989, Mount Redoubt erupted, spewing lava and ash for many miles. In December 1996, Mount Pavlof in the Aleutians erupted twice. This volcano sent ash clouds about six miles (10 km) into the sky. In 1997, more than seven hundred wildfires cut through forests, destroying almost 600,000 acres (242,811 hectares) of forestland. The environment continues to be a major concern for Alaskans, many of whom live close to nature in the Last Frontier.

Alaskans are trying to bridge the gap between its native and non-native people. In April 2001, Alaska Natives signed the historic Millennium Agreement with the Alaskan government. The agreement makes it possible for the state to work with Alaska's tribal governments. This could lead to improved public services for the tribal groups, such as better education and a cleaner environment. Alaskans are committed to working together to preserve both the people and the environment of this great land.

More than 2 million acres of Alaskan forest burned from wildfires during 1997, keeping firefighters busy.

CHAPTER FOUR

GOVERNING ALASKA

Alaska's state courthouse is across the street from the capitol building in Juneau.

The state of Alaska is governed according to its constitution, a document that outlines the rights of Alaska's citizens and determines how the state will be governed. Alaska's constitution was approved in 1956. Since then, it has been amended, or changed, many times to give more rights to its citizens and to better define its system of government.

Alaska's government has three branches, or parts, just like the United States government: the executive branch, the legislative branch, and the judicial branch. Executive refers to the leaders responsible for running the state and enforcing Alaska's laws. Legislative refers to people, called legislators, who make the laws. Judicial refers to judges and courts, where laws are interpreted to see if they are fair or not. In addition, there are several state departments that work closely with these branches. Together these three branches of government work together to run the state and enforce the laws.

EXECUTIVE BRANCH

The job of the executive branch is to enforce Alaska's laws. The executive branch is headed by the governor and lieutenant governor, who both serve four-year terms. The governor represents Alaska to other states and countries. He or she also determines how the state's money will be spent and appoints people to manage departments. These departments take care of issues such as environment conservation, military affairs, education, and health and social services. The lieutenant governor supervises elections and the Alaska Historical Commission, in addition to other duties.

Tony Knowles was governor of Alaska from 1994 to 2002. He stands with Fran Ulmer, who was his lieutenant governor.

LEGISLATIVE BRANCH

The legislative branch makes new laws and updates old laws. The legislature is made up of two houses: the senate and the house of representatives. There are twenty state senators, who serve four-year terms. Alaska's forty representatives serve two-year terms. Legislators meet every year for 120 days starting in January.

ALASKA GOVERNORS

Name	Term	Name	Term
William A. Egan	1959–1966	Bill Sheffield	1982–1986
Walter J. Hickel	1966–1969	Steve Cowper	1986–1990
Keith Miller	1969–1970	Walter J. Hickel	1990–1994
William A. Egan	1970–1974	Tony Knowles	1994–2002
Jay S. Hammond	1974–1982		

An idea for a law starts out as a bill and must be voted on by all the members of the legislature. If a majority of the legislators vote in favor of the bill, it is sent to the governor for signing. A bill only becomes a law if it has been signed by the governor. The governor has the right to veto, or reject, a law passed by the legislature; however, the legislature can also override his veto. Laws passed by the legislature may cover such topics as taxes, land use, and education.

JUDICIAL BRANCH

The job of the judicial branch is to make sure the state's laws follow the constitution and that Alaska's citizens are treated fairly regarding

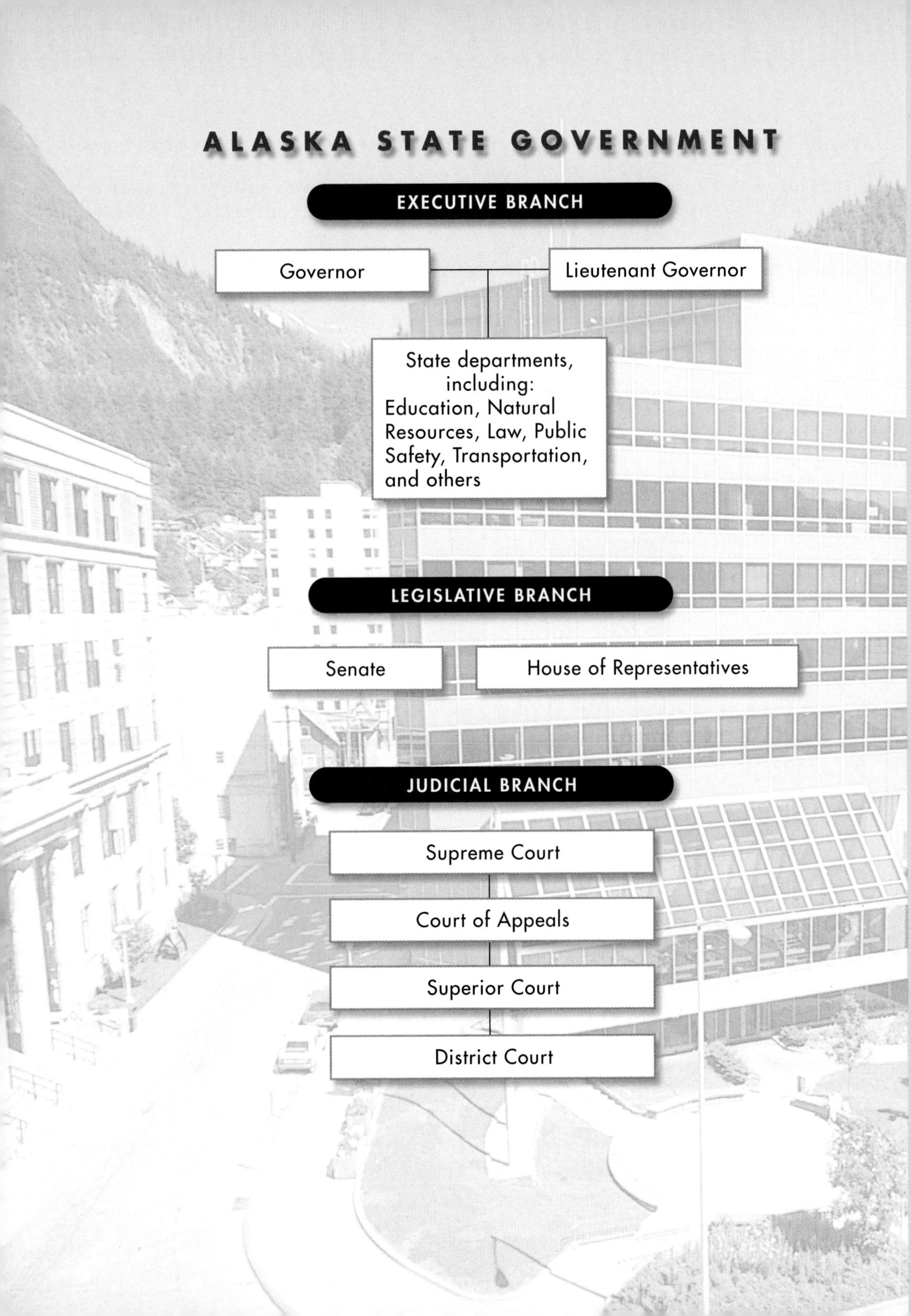

ALASKA STATE GOVERNMENT

EXECUTIVE BRANCH

Governor

Lieutenant Governor

State departments, including: Education, Natural Resources, Law, Public Safety, Transportation, and others

LEGISLATIVE BRANCH

Senate

House of Representatives

JUDICIAL BRANCH

Supreme Court

Court of Appeals

Superior Court

District Court

Alaska's laws. The judicial branch is made up of courts and judges. There are four levels of courts in Alaska: district courts, superior courts, a court of appeals, and the supreme court.

When a person is accused of breaking one of Alaska's laws, that person is given a trial in a district court. Judges make sure that the trial is conducted fairly. If one party is not satisfied with the court's decision, an appeal, or request for a new trial, is made to a higher court—either the superior court or a court of appeals. Alaska's highest court is the supreme court. It hears appeals from lower courts, and is also in charge of running the state's judicial system. The supreme court has four justices and one chief justice who serves a three-year term as administrator of the state judicial system.

TAKE A TOUR OF JUNEAU, THE STATE CAPITAL

When people say, "You can't get there from here," they could be talking about Juneau. Unlike other capital cities in the United States, Juneau has no roads leading to it. The city itself lies between Gastineau Channel and Mount Juneau, and visitors must fly in or take the Alaska Marine Highway ferry from the mainland. The city has about thirty thousand residents.

Although it may be hard to reach, Juneau's location is exactly what attracts tourists. It is near the Tongass Forest,

EXTRA! EXTRA!

In 1976, Alaskans voted to move the capital from Juneau to Willow, a city with a more central location. However, they changed their minds after finding out how expensive it would be to move the capital—more than $2 billion! Since then, other attempts have been made to move the capital or build a road leading to Juneau, but none have been successful.

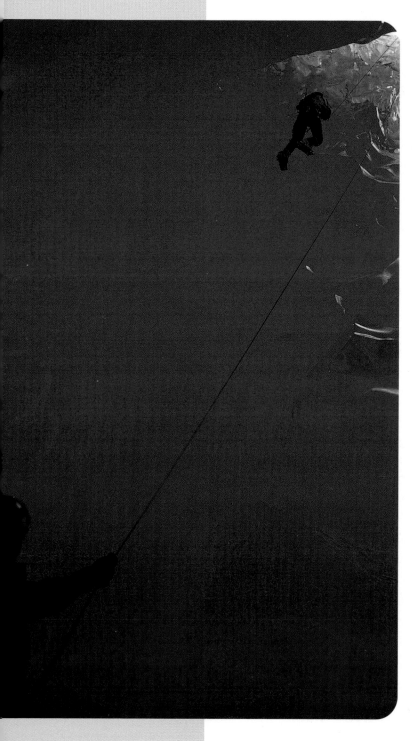

Mount Juneau and Mount Roberts, and Glacier Bay. Juneau is sometimes called the "Gateway to Glaciers" because of its nearness to the Lemon Creek Glacier, the Herbert Glacier, and the Mendenhall Glacier, which lies in the Tongass National Forest. The Mendenhall Glacier can be reached by car, and tourists may hike on trails above and beside the glacier. The East Glacier Trail offers a stunning view of Nugget Creek Falls.

Built in 1931, the state capitol stands in downtown Juneau. The brick and limestone building has four columns made of marble from Prince of Wales Island in Southeast Alaska. Alaskan scenes decorate walls inside the lobby. Carvings and sculptures depict major sources of income for the state, such as fishing, minerals, tourism, and hunting and trapping. The capitol contains offices for the governor and lieutenant governor, and meeting rooms for the senate and the house of representatives.

Nearby, the Juneau-Douglas City Museum records Juneau's mining history. It displays photographs and artifacts from early gold mining in the region. The Last Chance Mining Museum also portrays the story of gold mining through the use of maps showing mines, tunnels, and mine shafts.

At the Alaska State Museum, visitors learn all about the state's people and history. On display are Native Alaskan baskets, clothing, and masks. The museum also features a native clan house, and a totem pole with Abraham Lincoln's portrait carved into it. The main feature of the museum is an eagle's nest. Visitors can climb a circular stairway for a spectacular view. The recorded sounds of the eagles' calls make the experience very realistic.

If you're interested in Alaska's heritage, visit the House of Wickersham. This old Victorian house contains native crafts, artifacts, and photographs that were collected by Judge James Wickersham during his lifetime. Some of Juneau's most important residents lived in this house, including Frank Hammond, John Malony, and Bartlett Thane, all of whom were associated with the city's mining industry. Today, you can take a tour of the house in the summertime.

The Alaska state capitol was built in 1931.

(opposite)
Rappelling, a skill used in mountain climbing, is a popular activity on some of Alaska's glaciers. These climbers are rappelling within Mendenhall Glacier.

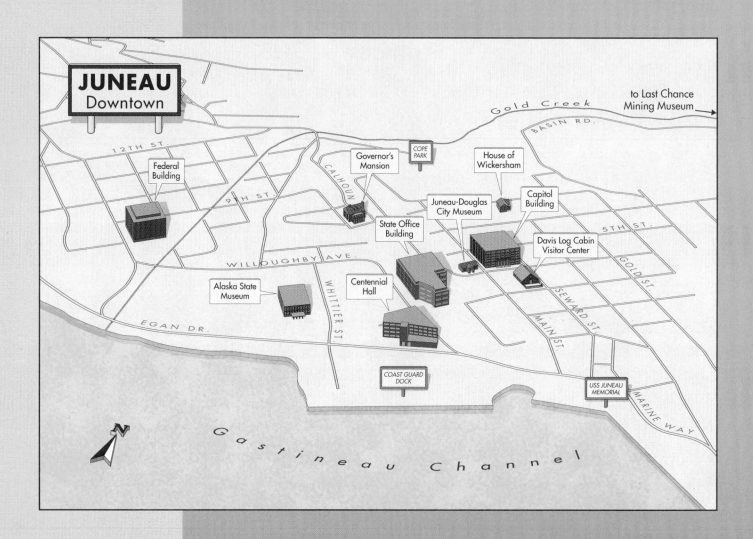

JUNEAU
Downtown

to Last Chance
Mining Museum

Gold Creek

BASIN RD.

12TH ST.

COPE
PARK

House of
Wickersham

Federal
Building

Governor's
Mansion

9TH ST.

CALHOUN

Juneau-Douglas
City Museum

Capitol
Building

5TH ST.

State Office
Building

Davis Log Cabin
Visitor Center

GOLD ST.

WILLOUGHBY AVE.

Alaska State
Museum

Centennial
Hall

SEWARD ST.

EGAN DR.

WHITTIER ST.

MAIN ST.

COAST GUARD
DOCK

USS JUNEAU
MEMORIAL

MARINE WAY

N

Gastineau Channel

If you're tired of walking, there's another great way to see Juneau—take a ride on the Mount Roberts Tramway. It's a 2,000-foot (610-m) ride up to the top of Mount Roberts, where you can get off and have a bite to eat in the restaurant or hike one of the many nature trails on the mountaintop. The views of Gastineau Channel and the surrounding mountains are spectacular.

The unique location of Juneau is best appreciated from a higher point of view.

CHAPTER FIVE

THE PEOPLE AND PLACES OF ALASKA

The Inupiat celebrate Nalukataq, the end of the whaling season, by playing the blanket toss.

More than 625,000 people live in Alaska—only Vermont and Wyoming have fewer people. Almost seven of every ten Alaskans are of European descent. More than three of every hundred are African-American, and four of every hundred are Asian. Most Alaskans live in cities. The state's largest city is Anchorage, followed by Fairbanks and Juneau.

ALASKA NATIVES

About sixteen of every hundred people in Alaska are Alaska Natives. Three main groups live there: the Inuit, the Aleuts, and Alaskan Indians. In all, there are about 94,000 native people living in Alaska.

The Inuit were formerly called Eskimos. The word *eskimo* is an Algonquian word meaning "eaters of raw meat." The Eskimos actually call themselves Inupiat, or Yupik, which means "real people." The main Arctic-region towns in which the Inupiat live are Barrow, Kotzebue, Nome, Gambell, and Savoonga. The Yupik people live in western Alaska. Bethel is the largest Yupik town. Inupiat and Yupik also live on remote islands in the Bering Sea, such as Little Diomede, St. Lawrence, and Nunivak.

Although they are often associated with igloos, Inuit people do not really live in homes made of ice. The word *iglu*, which means "house" in Inuit, comes from eastern Eskimos who live in Canada. An iglu is temporary housing used only while traveling—an ice motel, so to speak. Today, people live in more modern housing.

The Aleut live on the Aleutian Islands. In past times, the Aleut sailed in small, skin-covered sea kayaks called *baidarkas*. In those boats, the Aleut traveled hundreds of miles into the Bering Sea or

This photo shows an Inuit village in Alaska.

Alaska Natives perform traditional dances for a crowd.

northern Pacific Ocean in search of whales, walruses, or seals. The Aleut are known for weaving grass or reed baskets of unusual beauty and strength. Original Aleut baskets are displayed in Alaskan museums and are extremely valuable.

The Athabascan, Tlingit, Haida, and Tsimshian tribes make up the Alaskan Indian tribes. There are about thirty-one thousand Alaskan Indians. It is thought that the ancestors of these people moved to Alaska from Canada or from the Pacific Northwest. The Athabascan live mostly in the Interior. The Tlingit, Haida, and Tsimshian live on Alaska's Panhandle.

Alaskans make a major effort to preserve their native heritage. The Naa Kahidi Theater and the Cape Fox Dancers, both in Saxman, and the Chilkat Dancers in Haines perform songs and dances of the Tlingit, Haida, and Tsimshian tribes. They present their customs, history, and legends through art. In the same way, Inuit present their history at the Living Museum of the Arctic in Kotzebue through stories, songs, and dances.

FIND OUT MORE

Totem poles are tall, carved and painted logs that record the history of a family or clan through sculptures of birds, animals, fish, whales, and other things. Some have faces of evil spirits; others have plants drawn on them. If you carved a totem pole to represent your family, what would it show?

EDUCATION

Alaskans are among the best-educated people in the country. They have the third-highest graduation rate in the United States—nine of every ten Alaskans twenty-five years or older are high school graduates.

Before 1976, there were no high schools in Alaska's remote villages. As a result, many high school students often had to travel long distances to attend school, or live away from home in a boarding school. In 1976, sixteen-year-old Alaska Native Molly Hootch and other students won a class action suit against the Alaska Board of Education, which resulted in the Molly Hootch Decree. This decree forced the state to provide a high school in any community with at least one high-school-age student. More than one hundred villages became eligible for high schools under this program.

About one-fourth of Alaskan adults hold college degrees. The University of Alaska has main campuses in Fairbanks, Anchorage, and Juneau, as well as many other branches throughout the

Inupiat children learn to use computers at school.

WHO'S WHO IN ALASKA?

Sheldon Jackson (1834–1909) was a missionary who worked to improve the educational and economic well-being of the people of Alaska. He was the first General Agent of Education in Alaska and opened public schools for Alaska Native children. He also collected native artifacts that are today housed in the Sheldon Jackson Museum in Sitka. He was born in New York and lived for many years in Alaska.

state. Other universities and colleges include Alaska Pacific University and Sheldon Jackson College.

WORKING IN ALASKA

Service Industry

Many Alaskans work in service businesses, such as hotels, motels, health care, and restaurants. Transportation is also an important service industry for the state, since pipelines and shipping are a necessity for bringing in and sending out goods. Government services include operating public schools, public hospitals, and military bases. Most of the service industries are located around urban centers, particularly Fairbanks, Anchorage, and Juneau. About four of every ten Alaskans hold service jobs.

Much of the king crab catch comes from the water surrounding the Aleutian Islands.

Fishing

Alaska ranks first in the United States in commercial fishing. Despite its importance, the fishing industry does not employ many people, and the fishing season can be quite short. For example, the crab fishing season is only about one month long. Some of the fish and seafood caught in Alaska are salmon, king crab, herring, halibut, shrimp, scallops, and pollock. Kodiak and Unalaska are the state's major fishing ports.

Pollock is a type of fish belonging to the codfish family. It is harvested in the cold, clear waters of Alaska's Bering Sea and the Gulf of Alaska. The recipe below is an easy and delicious way to prepare pollock; be sure to ask an adult for help!

MEXICAN-STYLE ALASKAN POLLOCK

(serves 4)
4 fillets pollock or other white fish
1 teaspoon chili powder
1 teaspoon parsley, dried
2 cups corn meal
spray-on pan release
prepared salsa

1. Heat oven to 450°F.
2. Spray an oven-proof baking dish with spray-on pan release.
3. Mix corn meal, parsley, and chili powder in a shallow dish.
4. Wash each fillet in water, then coat each side by pressing it into the corn meal.
5. Bake 8-12 minutes, until coating is light brown and fish is flaky. Test fish with fork.
6. Serve topped with 1-2 tablespoons of salsa.

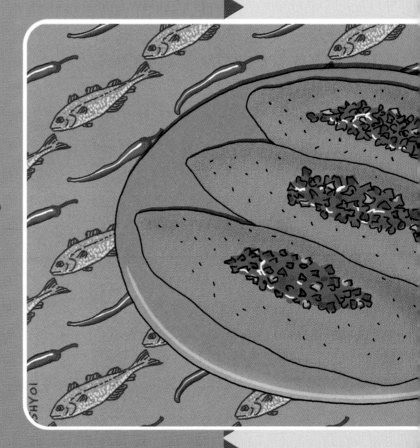

Commercial fish processing in Alaska is a one-stop event. Processors and packagers set out to sea on huge ships. As fish are caught, people known as processors clean and fillet the fish. Packagers then place the fish into boxes, and the product is frozen. The giant processor ships return to port only when their freezers are full.

Commercial fishing rules determine the amount of fish caught each year. This is controlled according to time periods or by the number of fish caught. For example, crab fishing is limited to four to six weeks each year, and much of the catch is sold long before it leaves the water. Halibut, on the other hand, has a quota (limit) set by the number of pounds caught. In 1997, the halibut quota was fifty-one million pounds.

Commercial fishing is a big business in Alaska for a few months each year. Fishermen often live on their ships for up to three months at a time.

FIND OUT MORE

A salmon dinner for a family of six uses about two pounds (1 kg) of fish. In one year, the Alaskan salmon catch equals about 900 million pounds. How many family dinners would 900 million pounds of fish feed?

Mining

Alaska is rich in natural resources. Oil, natural gas, and other mineral resources provide a large part of Alaska's income. In spite of their importance, however, these industries do not employ many people—only about four of every one hundred workers are miners.

Oil and natural gas are found in huge deposits on the North Slope. The largest producing wells are at Point McIntyre, North Prudhoe Bay, and Niakuk. Other oil areas in Alaska are on the Kenai Peninsula and in Cook Inlet. The huge amounts of oil are transported to other states in oil tankers or through the Trans-Alaska Pipeline.

This oil refinery is at Prudhoe Bay, an area that is rich in oil.

Gold, silver, coal, copper, molybdenum, platinum, tin, zinc, and mercury are abundant in Alaska. Gold is mined along the Yukon River, on the Seward Peninsula, and in the Alaska Panhandle. Copper is found along the Copper River in the Wrangell Mountain Range. Iron ore is found along the Klondike border with Canada, and tin is mined in the district of Nome. The largest producer of zinc in the world is the Red Dog Mine in northwest Alaska.

Agriculture and Forestry

Only a small portion of Alaska land is used for farming. There are more than five hundred farms in the state. The growing season is short because of Alaska's climate.

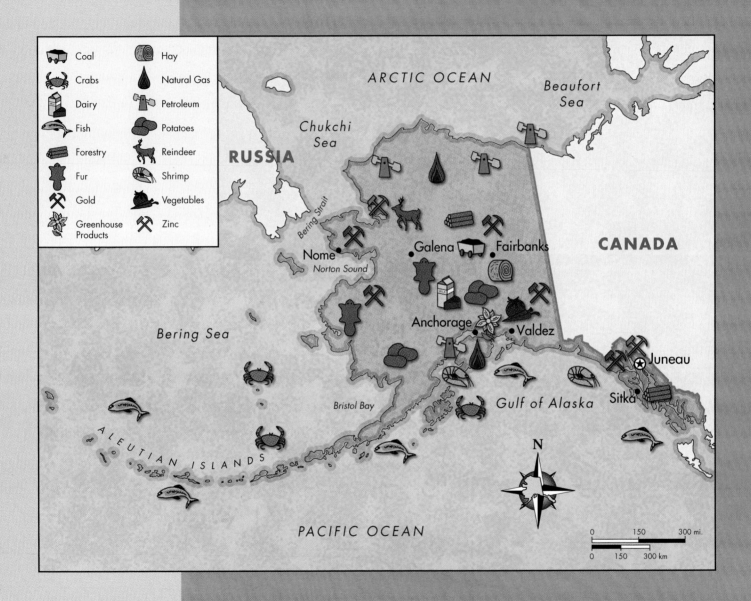

Coal		Hay	
Crabs		Natural Gas	
Dairy		Petroleum	
Fish		Potatoes	
Forestry		Reindeer	
Fur		Shrimp	
Gold		Vegetables	
Greenhouse Products		Zinc	

ARCTIC OCEAN

Beaufort Sea

Chukchi Sea

RUSSIA

CANADA

Bering Strait

Galena

Fairbanks

Nome

Norton Sound

Bering Sea

Anchorage

Valdez

Juneau

Bristol Bay

Gulf of Alaska

Sitka

A L E U T I A N   I S L A N D S

N

PACIFIC OCEAN

0	150	300 mi.
0	150	300 km

The main farm products are eggs, milk, feed for animals, potatoes, summer vegetables, and greenhouse products, or plants and vegetables grown in protective houses. Some Alaskan farmers also grow barley, hay, and oats. Most farm products grow in the Matanuska Valley, just north of Anchorage, or in the Tanana Valley, near Fairbanks and Delta. There are also a number of farms for raising livestock, including sheep, beef cattle, horses, and the not-so-common reindeer. Reindeer is a subsistence food for many Alaska Natives.

Much of Alaska's logging industry takes place in the southeastern part of the state, with centers in Ketchikan and Sitka.

Some Alaskans work in the wood products industry. Alaska's forests provide wood for pulp and lumber. Most saleable lumber is found in Southeast Alaska's forests. Wood pulp is used for making paper and cardboard. The state's biggest customer for raw wood and lumber is Japan because Japan has very little timber of its own.

Alaska has laws that limit the amount of timber cutting. This is a way of conserving natural forests. Because of these strict laws, there are only about twenty sawmills in the state.

Tourism

Alaska has a booming tourist industry. Tourism—the business of providing food, shelter, and entertainment for visitors—brings in about $900 million of income for the state each year. Cruise ships are especially popular, particularly those that travel Glacier Bay. The state has several large national parks, including Wrangell-St. Elias, Denali, Kenai, and Katmai. Fishing, wildlife, and rugged mountains are Alaska's chief attractions. Cold weather, however, isn't popular with tourists—visitors usually plan trips in July and August, when camping and fishing are at their peak, and there's little chance of snow.

EXTRA! EXTRA!

Alaska has plenty to be proud of, including having the "most" or the "largest" of many things. Here are just a few:

- The largest United States National Park is Wrangell-St. Elias, east of Anchorage.
- The largest known nesting group of bald eagles in the world lives along the Chilkat River.
- More than 120 million seabirds, such as gulls, terns, ducks, and sandpipers, nest in Alaska each summer—more than the number of seabirds in all the other states combined.
- Alaska has more private pilots and more planes per person than any other state.
- Lake Hood is the world's largest seaplane base, where more than eight hundred landings and take-offs occur on an average summer day.
- El Cap Pit is the deepest natural cave in the United States, plunging 598 feet (182 m).

TAKE A TOUR OF ALASKA

Touring Alaska can be a rugged camping and hiking adventure, a spectacular drive through natural wonders, or a luxury cruise—whichever you prefer. There is plenty to see and do. Just bring hiking boots, camera film, and lots of insect repellent—there are between twenty-five and forty types of mosquitoes in Alaska. Some are so large, locals jokingly call them the "state bird."

The Panhandle

Sitka is located on Baranof Island, one of a string of islands in the Alaska Panhandle. For tourists, Sitka is close to Glacier Bay, Ketchikan, Juneau, and Skagway. With its picturesque harbor, mountains, and forests, it is considered Alaska's most beautiful seaside town.

Sitka is a small, yet beautiful, seaside community.

Sitka was founded by Russian Alexandr Baranov and was originally called New Archangel. One of the interesting sites in Sitka is the Russian Bishop's House. In 1842, the Russian America Company built the Bishop's House for Father Veniaminov, later called Bishop Innocent. The original house is now part of the national park system. Nearby is St. Michael's Russian Orthodox Cathedral, first built in 1848. After a fire in 1966, the church was rebuilt according to the original plans.

Bird lovers will enjoy visiting the Alaska Raptor Rehabilitation Center, where injured eagles, hawks, owls, and falcons are cared for. Farther up the Panhandle, north of Juneau, is Chilkat Bald Eagle Preserve, home to more than 3,500 bald eagles.

West of Juneau is Glacier Bay National Park. The park is an amazing expanse of natural environment that includes, besides the two arms of

It's a spectacular sight to watch large pieces of ice calving, or splitting off, from a glacier.

the bay, snow-capped mountains, glaciers, islands, and coastal beaches. There are plenty of outdoor activities at the park, from kayaking and rafting to camping and hiking. Nearby Tongass National Forest also offers spectacular scenery and outdoor adventure.

If you'd rather relax, take a cruise of Glacier Bay. If you're lucky you might catch of glimpse of "calving"—the splitting off of pieces of glacier. You might also see a pod of orcas glide through the waves or catch a glimpse of a humpback whale's spout.

Anchorage, Denali, and Fairbanks

Visitors to Anchorage enjoy museums, galleries, and tourist attractions. At the Alaska Experience Theater, you can watch a forty-minute film about Alaska on a giant circular screen. Another exhibit, called the Safe-Quake Theatre, offers a way to experience earthquakes in a virtual format. The Anchorage Museum of History and Art features displays of native art and Alaska history. Other places of interest include the Captain Cook Monument, commemorating the 200th anniversary of Captain James Cook's exploration of the area, and Nesbett State Courthouse. Two large totem poles, erected in 1997, stand in front of the Nesbett State Courthouse.

Ride the train north to Denali National Park, which surrounds North America's tallest mountain, Denali. Originally founded in 1917 as McKinley National Park, Denali is a nature lover's paradise. Park visitors snap photos of moose, grizzly bears, eagles, and caribou. The animals are truly wild, and there is enough habitat in Denali to support their needs. Feeding the residents is not allowed—they have plenty of food growing in the park.

Just north of Denali is Fairbanks. Visitors will want to see Pioneer Park, a city park with an all-Alaska feel to it. Pioneer Park presents the rugged pioneer life of the state during the 1800s and early 1900s. Within the park is the Pioneer Museum, which has a model Alaska Native village, the S.S. *Nenana* riverboat, and a log cabin village. While in Fairbanks, visitors can check out the University of Alaska Museum and the Georgeson Botanical Garden and Experimental Farm. The museum features exhibits on the history of Alaska,

Anchorage is like any other American city, with apartments, malls, tall buildings, restaurants, and even traffic jams.

The Chena River winds through the middle of Fairbanks.

Alaska Natives, and wildlife. The Botanical Garden highlights the native plants of Alaska. The Experimental Farm's scientists try to uncover new techniques for growing crops in Alaska's short growing season.

Another stop on the tour is Wrangell-St. Elias National Park and Preserve, the largest national park in the United States. It covers more than thirteen million acres, which is an area larger than Connecticut, Rhode Island, and Massachusetts combined. The park includes the Malaspina Glacier to the south of Mount St. Elias, and the Columbus Icefield, directly north of the mountain.

Along the Aleutians

The Aleutians provide many marvelous sights. Katmai National Park and the Valley of Ten Thousand Smokes provided the site of one of the greatest volcanic eruptions in history—that of Novarupta in 1912. Volcanic ash up to seven hundred feet (214 m) deep buried the plants and animals living there, changing the landscape forever. Across the water is Kodiak National Wildlife Refuge, a state park in which visitors can see Kodiak bears.

A ferry ride away from Kodiak is Kenai National Wildlife Refuge and Kenai Fjords National Park. This region is rugged, remarkably beautiful, and surprisingly close to Anchorage, Alaska's largest city. Visitors to Kenai can paddle kayaks, laugh at the antics of sea otters, and admire soaring eagles. Hikers in Kenai National Wildlife Refuge should be prepared to meet moose and brown bears.

Western Alaska

Nome, which began as a mining town in the late 1800s, is on the Seward Peninsula in western Alaska. It was once the largest city in Alaska. Today, Nome has about 3,500 residents.

Alaskan moose are the largest in all of North America and can be found in Kenai National Wildlife Refuge.

Nome is the finish line for the Iditarod. "End of the trail" festivities are celebrated during the entire month of March, including arts and crafts shows, dart tournaments, reindeer potluck dinners, and slide shows. One of the more famous festivities is also one of the world's most unusual—the Bering Sea Ice Golf Classic. This annual golf game, also played in March, takes place on the frozen waters of the Bering Sea. Don't worry if you don't get there in March—there's something going on almost every month in Nome!

A trip to the bush helps a visitor really understand how many Alaskan people live. Alaska has hundreds of very small villages, populated mostly by Alaska Natives who may live traditional lifestyles.

Kipnuk is a Yupik village near the ocean located in the Kuskokwim delta region in western Alaska. About 470 people live there. You can get to Kipnuk by a small plane that leaves from Bethel and stops at several other villages along the way. Kipnuk's airport consists of a small landing

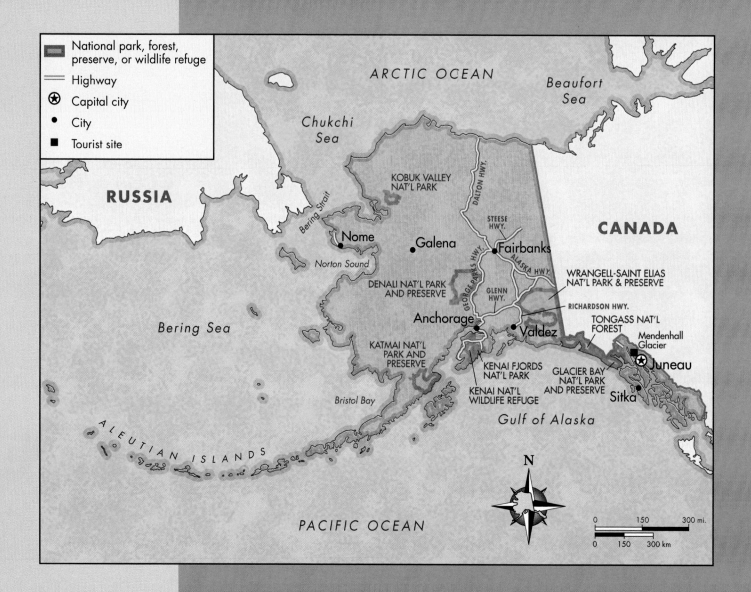

National park, forest, preserve, or wildlife refuge

Highway

Capital city

City

Tourist site

ARCTIC OCEAN

Beaufort Sea

Chukchi Sea

RUSSIA

Bering Strait

KOBUK VALLEY NAT'L PARK

DALTON HWY.

STEESE HWY.

CANADA

Nome

Galena

Fairbanks

Norton Sound

GEORGE PARKS HWY.

ALASKA HWY.

WRANGELL-SAINT ELIAS NAT'L PARK & PRESERVE

DENALI NAT'L PARK AND PRESERVE

GLENN HWY.

RICHARDSON HWY.

Bering Sea

Anchorage

Valdez

TONGASS NAT'L FOREST

Mendenhall Glacier

KATMAI NAT'L PARK AND PRESERVE

KENAI FJORDS NAT'L PARK

GLACIER BAY NAT'L PARK AND PRESERVE

Juneau

Bristol Bay

KENAI NAT'L WILDLIFE REFUGE

Sitka

Gulf of Alaska

ALEUTIAN ISLANDS

N

PACIFIC OCEAN

0   150   300 mi.

0   150   300 km

EXTRA! EXTRA!

A world-famous sled dog race called the Iditarod takes place every year in March. The route covers 1,049 miles (1,688 km) from Anchorage to Nome. It follows the route of a famous 1925 trip to deliver vaccine during an outbreak of diphtheria, a deadly disease caused by bacteria. This race challenges dog teams and their owners, as they race through high winds, blizzards, and below-freezing temperatures. The first Iditarod, called the Last Great Race on Earth, was run in 1973.

strip and a small wooden building. The largest building in town is the school, a modern one-story building for grades kindergarten to twelve. Boardwalks around the school lead to houses, a combined store and post office, and to the churches in town. The boardwalks make it easy to walk over the spongy tundra. There are no cars in Kipnuk, just four wheelers and snowmobiles, because there are no roads and no place to drive a car.

The land is very flat, and you'll be able to see for long distances. If you are lucky, you might be invited into someone's home. You might be surprised to learn that some houses do not have running water or indoor plumbing. Kipnuk is so remote that it must generate its own electricity. However, the school is equipped with modern computers, and people have satellite televisions.

In spring and fall, the ground in Kipnuk often becomes so wet that it is impassable without boardwalks.

Northern Alaska

From Fairbanks, daring visitors might drive the Dalton Highway to northern Alaska. The highway was built specifically for supply trucks during the construction of the northern section of the Trans-Alaska Pipeline. This highway is rugged and remote, and crosses the Arctic Circle, the Yukon River, and Brooks Range. It also passes near the Gates of the Arctic National Park and the Yukon Flats Wildlife Preserve, where massive herds of caribou move over land that few people have ever seen.

The northernmost town in the United States is Barrow, located on the Arctic Ocean just 1,300 miles (2,092 km) from the North Pole. Barrow has a population of 4,581, most of whom are Inupiat. It is the main town on the North Slope. Despite its far-north location, Barrow has all

The Dalton Highway is known by Alaskans as "the haul road" because it serves trucks maintaining the Trans-Alaska Pipeline.

the common conveniences of modern life. Students enjoy pop music and video games. Families shop in supermarkets and over the Internet.

Barrow is a small city with modern conveniences.

Your tour around Alaska has taken you by ferry, train, car, and bush plane. You have visited a United States capital with whales in its backyard, a large city that is a worldwide airline hub, and an isolated native village. You saw the highest peak in North America, glaciers, rivers, and tundra wildflowers. These are just a few of the things that make Alaskans proud of their unique state—the Last Frontier.

ALASKA ALMANAC

Statehood date and number: January 3, 1959, 49th state

State seal: The Great Seal of Alaska shows the beauty and wealth of the state. The aurora borealis shines above rugged mountains. In the foreground are symbols of farming, fishing, and transportation. Adopted: 1913.

State flag: The flag is a dark blue background with the North Star shown above the Big Dipper. Adopted, 1927.

Geographic center: 63°50' N by 152°W

Total area/rank: 615,230 square miles (1,593,438 sq km)/1st

Coastline: 33,904 miles (54,563 km)

Borders: Canada, Gulf of Alaska, Pacific Ocean, Bering Sea, Arctic Ocean, Chukchi Sea, Russia (across Bering Strait)

Latitude and longitude: Approximately 52°00' and 74°00'N by 130°00' to 172°E

Highest/lowest elevation: Denali (Mt. McKinley), 20,320 feet (6,194 m)/sea level

Hottest/coldest temperature: 100°F (38°C) at Fort Yukon on June 27, 1915/–80°F (–62°C) at Prospect Creek on January 23, 1971

Land area/rank: 570,374 square miles (1,477,269 sq km)/1st

Inland water/rank: 44,856 square miles (sq km)/1st

Population/rank: 626,932 (2000 Census)/48th

Population of major cities:

Anchorage: 260,283

Juneau: 30,711

Fairbanks: 30,224

Origin of state name: Aleut word *Alyeska* (al-ay-es-ka) or "great land"

State capital: Juneau, named capital in 1900

Boroughs: 16

State government: Twenty senators, forty representatives

Major rivers/ lakes: Yukon, Porcupine, Koyukuk, Tanana, Innoko, Colville, Noatak, Kobuk, Birch Creek, Chilkat, Nushagak, and Naknek/lakes: Iliamna, Becharof, Teshekpuk, Naknek, Clark, Tustumena, Dall, Upper Ugashik, Lower Ugashik, and Kukaklek

Farm products: Eggs, milk, hay, greenhouse plants, potatoes, and lumber

Livestock: Cattle/calves and hogs/pigs

Manufactured products: Petroleum products, processed fish, wood products, and paper products

Mining products: Gold, silver, zinc, stone, platinum, lead, gems, petroleum, and coal

Fishing products: Crab, salmon, shrimp, scallops, clams, herring, and pollock

Bird: Willow ptarmigan

Fish: King salmon

Flower: Forget-me-not

Folk dance: Square dancing

Fossil: Woolly mammoth

Gem: Jade

Marine mammal: Bowhead whale

Mineral: Gold

Motto: North to the Future

Nickname: Last Frontier, Land of the Midnight Sun, Great Land

Song: "Alaska's Flag," words by Marie Drake, music by Elinor Dusenbury. Adopted: 1955

Sport: Dog mushing

Tree: Sitka spruce

Wildlife: black bears, grizzly bears, polar bears, Kodiak bears, American bison, caribou, reindeer, Sitka deer, Roosevelt elk, moose, mountain goats, musk oxen, Dall sheep, wolves, wolverines, beavers, foxes, lynx, martens, muskrats, otters, raccoons, squirrels, weasels, deer mice, tundra hares, snowshoe hares, picas, porcupines, various whales, seals, walruses, and dolphins. Birds: ducks, geese, swans, Arctic terns, bald eagles, Arctic falcons, American falcons, Peale's falcons, Eskimo curlews, Steller's eider ducks, Arctic warblers, bluethroats, emperor geese, horned puffins, and Pacific loons. Fish: salmon, shrimp, king crab, Dungeness crab, herring, halibut, pollock, Arctic char, burbot, cutthroat trout, kokanee, rainbow trout, and white fish

TIMELINE

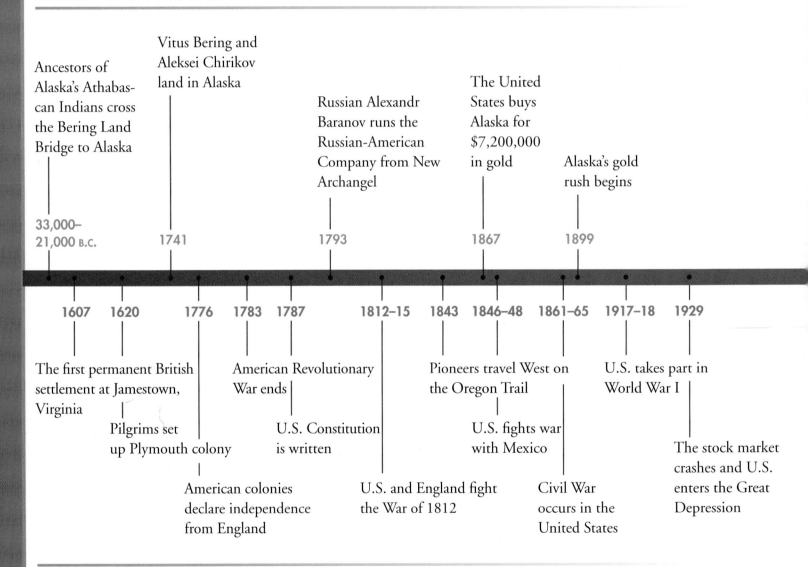

Ancestors of Alaska's Athabascan Indians cross the Bering Land Bridge to Alaska

33,000–21,000 B.C.

Vitus Bering and Aleksei Chirikov land in Alaska

1741

Russian Alexandr Baranov runs the Russian-American Company from New Archangel

1793

The United States buys Alaska for $7,200,000 in gold

1867

Alaska's gold rush begins

1899

1607   1620   1776   1783   1787   1812–15   1843   1846–48   1861–65   1917–18   1929

The first permanent British settlement at Jamestown, Virginia

Pilgrims set up Plymouth colony

American colonies declare independence from England

American Revolutionary War ends

U.S. Constitution is written

U.S. and England fight the War of 1812

Pioneers travel West on the Oregon Trail

U.S. fights war with Mexico

Civil War occurs in the United States

U.S. takes part in World War I

The stock market crashes and U.S. enters the Great Depression

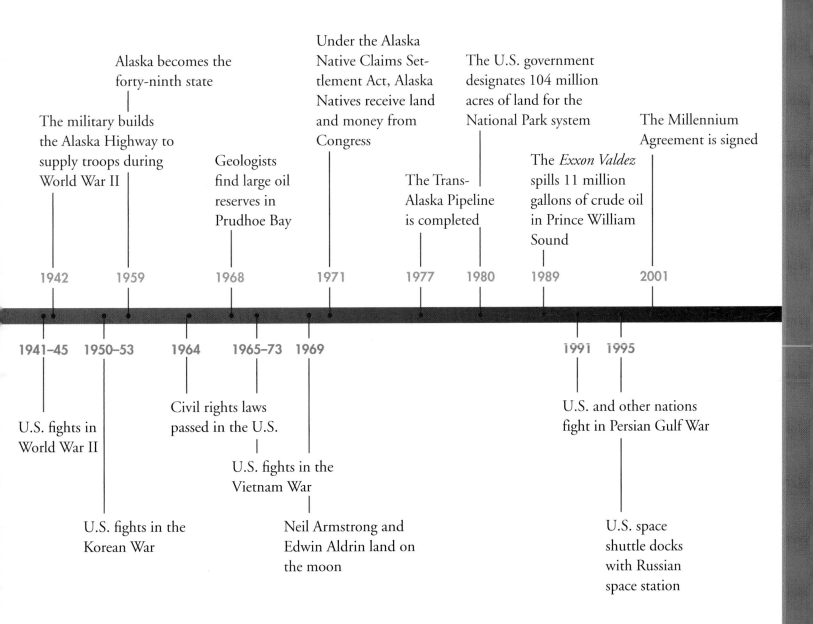

Alaska becomes the
forty-ninth state

Under the Alaska
Native Claims Set-
tlement Act, Alaska
Natives receive land
and money from
Congress

The U.S. government
designates 104 million
acres of land for the
National Park system

The Millennium
Agreement is signed

The military builds
the Alaska Highway to
supply troops during
World War II

Geologists
find large oil
reserves in
Prudhoe Bay

The Trans-
Alaska Pipeline
is completed

The *Exxon Valdez*
spills 11 million
gallons of crude oil
in Prince William
Sound

1942   1959   1968   1971   1977   1980   1989   2001

1941–45   1950–53   1964   1965–73   1969   1991   1995

Civil rights laws
passed in the U.S.

U.S. and other nations
fight in Persian Gulf War

U.S. fights in
World War II

U.S. fights in the
Vietnam War

U.S. fights in the
Korean War

Neil Armstrong and
Edwin Aldrin land on
the moon

U.S. space
shuttle docks
with Russian
space station

GALLERY OF FAMOUS ALASKANS

Susan Butcher
(1954–)
The first person to win three Iditarod races in a row, in 1986, 1987, and 1988; she also won the race in 1990. Butcher is an experienced dog musher and trainer. She lives in Eureka.

Ernest Gruening
(1887–1974)
The first territorial governor of Alaska and a leader in the effort to gain Alaska statehood. In 1959, he became one of Alaska's first United States senators.

Katie John
(1915–)
A Yupik woman who sued the state of Alaska to maintain the right to live the subsistence lifestyle.

Joseph Juneau
(1826?–1890)
A gold prospector who made the first major discovery of gold in Alaska, near Juneau. The city is named after him.

Jewel Kilcher
(1974–)
A popular singer and songwriter, known as Jewel.

She grew up on a homestead in Homer, Alaska.

Sydney M. Laurence
(1865–1940)
A well–known painter from Alaska. He painted a variety of Alaskan scenes, in particular those of Denali and the Alaskan wilderness. He was born in Brooklyn, New York, and later moved to Alaska.

Margaret Murie
(1902–)
"Grandmother" of environmentalism. She played a key role in the passing of the Wilderness Act and the Alaska Lands Act, which set aside parks, refuges, and preserves in Alaska. Born in Seattle and lived for several years in Fairbanks.

Howard Rock
(1911–1976)
An Inupiat statesman who founded the *Tundra Times*, Alaska's native newspaper, and helped to craft the Alaska Native Claims Act. Rock was also a world renowned artist.

Velma Wallis
(1960–)
A contemporary writer who won the Western Book Award for her novel, *Two Old Women*. She is an Athabascan and lives near Fairbanks.

GLOSSARY

amendment: change in a law or document

aurora borealis: lights in the northern night sky caused by the glowing of electrical energy

constitution: basic rules and laws that run a government

czar: the name for emperors who ruled Russia before 1917

glacier: ancient, large body of ice formed from closely packed snow

governor: an elected person who leads a state

legislature: a group of people who make laws

lichens: fungus and algae that grow and spread over rocks and tree trunks, and look somewhat like moss

paleo-Indians: early or "old" native people, who lived before written history began

peninsula: a body of land surrounded on three sides by water

permafrost: soil that is permanently frozen

sound: a long stretch of water separating an island from the mainland

strait: a narrow body of water joining two larger bodies of water

territory: land that is ruled or governed by a country. A United States territory is run by Congress, but does not have the same rights as a state

tsunami: a tidal wave created by an earthquake

tundra: treeless land usually found near the Arctic Circle or at higher elevations

FOR MORE INFORMATION

Web sites

State of Alaska Online

www.state.ak.us/

The state government's main Web site

Alaska Tourism for Students

www.dced.state.ak.us/tourism/student.htm

Student information about Alaska

Yahooligans! in Alaska

www.yahooligans.com/Around_the_World/U_S_States/ Alaska/

ThinkQuest entries from kids in Alaska

Books

Brown, Tricia. *Children of the Midnight Sun: Young Native Voices of Alaska.* Anchorage, AK: Alaska Northwest Books, 1998.

Haigh, Jane G., and Claire Rudolf Murphy. *Children of the Gold Rush.* New York, NY: Roberts Rinehart Publishers, 1999.

Hoyt-Goldsmith, Diane. *Potlatch: A Tsimshian Celebration.* New York, NY: Holiday House, 1997.

Levinson, Nancy Smiler, and Byrn Barnard. *If You Lived in the Alaska Territory.* New York, NY: Scholastic, 1998.

Paul, Frances Lackey. *Kahtahah: A Tlingit Girl.* Anchorage, AK: Alaska Northwest Books, 1996.

Addresses

Anchorage Convention and Visitors Bureau

524 W. Fourth Avenue
Anchorage, AK 99501

Alaska State Chamber of Commerce

217 Second Street, Suite 201
Juneau, AK 99801

Alaska State Park Information

3601 C Street, Suite 200
Anchorage, AK 99503-5929

Office of the Governor

P.O. Box 110001
Juneau, AK 99811

INDEX

MEET THE AUTHOR

Barbara A. Somervill is fascinated by Alaska. To find information about Alaska she checked a number of sources: the Internet, Chambers of Commerce and tourist bureaus, and the local library. One of the most interesting books Barbara found was *The Alaska Almanac*, published by Alaska Northwest Books. Barbara was raised and educated in New York State. She's also lived in Toronto, Canada; Canberra, Australia; Palo Alto, California; and South Carolina. She is the mother of four boys, two dogs, and a cat; and the proud grandmother of Lilly.